MW00744670

REMARKABLE SERVICE

Published by:
90-Minute Books
302 Martinique Drive
Winter Haven, FL 33884
www.90minutebooks.com

Published in the United States of America

ISBN-13: 978-0692602928
ISBN-10: 0692602925

For more information on 90-Minute Books, visit www.90minutebooks.com
or call (863) 318-0464.

Here Is What's Inside...

"We see our customers as invited guests to a party, and we are the hosts. It's our job every day to make every important aspect of the customer service experience a little bit better."
-Jeff Bezos, Amazon

Introduction

Over the years, people have asked me many questions about Customer Service: *What is Remarkable Service? How can our business improve so that everyone's talking about our service?* Is customer service that big of a deal? It's my hope that this book will offer a unique perspective on these questions and the topic of *Remarkable Service*, which I am very passionate about.

As a young man, I was fortunate to learn two valuable lessons from my parents. My father taught me to work hard, and my mother taught me to be nice. A great combination for life skills, I think. Little did I know at that time how valuable those lessons would become in my life and career.

When I was a teenager, I lived and worked in a small town: Minton, Saskatchewan, Canada. I learned at a very young age the importance of providing great customer service at my first job as a Parts Department Assistant at a small farm equipment dealership called Hibbard Equipment. Most of our customers were farmers living in Canada and the U.S.A., as we were close to the border of both countries. Many customers were demanding because they needed service and parts to repair broken-down farm equipment that was vital to their livelihoods. Time was often of the essence so that they could do their farming when the weather was favourable. In fact, it wasn't uncommon for them to give me a call at 11:00 at night or 5:00 in the morning, requesting me to go down to the "shop" to help them purchase a part to repair their broken equipment. I always regarded it as my "duty and obligation" because I was paid to deliver good customer service. (I didn't know at the time whether it was *remarkable* or not, but I did know that it was important!) As I became more experienced, I got to know many customers, and it was evident that most of them genuinely appreciated the support and service. While it was on a small scale, customer service became ingrained in my DNA, and has remained that way throughout my career. I learned that **when you treat customers well and show them respect, they usually come back**. What a concept!!!

The reality is that all of us appreciate being treated well when we're customers. Perhaps the cashier at the local grocery store waves you ahead in the line, or your car is just a little extra shiny after you pick it up from a service. We want it, we hope for it, and we expect it.

After starting my business, X5 Management, in 2006, I knew that customer service was a vital component of retaining our customers. Keeping customers happy may eventually earn us the right to ask for a referral, or gain more business. In the early years of my business, I put a greater focus of my energy into improving sales for our customers (i.e. sales coaching, training, and consulting). While customer service was important, more customers looked for us to support them with improving sales—growth in sales, put more sales in the pipeline, a higher volume of new customers for their businesses, etc. While this was valuable for our customers, we found there was much more to offer them as part of our service. Regardless of how well the economy is doing or what the price of oil is at any given time, **Customer Service is the one thing** that any business can control and improve upon 24/7, 365 days a year, but it's all about progress, not perfection! You can't fix everything in your business in one swoop. It takes time and patience, requiring constant and never-ending improvement.

In my opinion, many businesses don't put enough focus, attention, and effort into their customer service. I want to bring more awareness to businesses that can make their customer service experiences better and, ideally, *remarkable*. I also want businesses to feel great about it in the process. While I can think of several examples of truly *Remarkable Service*, unfortunately, I can think of many more that aren't so good. Ultimately, as customers, we expect more, and we deserve more, and YOUR customers think the same way.

I hope this book creates greater awareness of the value of creating *remarkable* customer service, offers suggestions to improve, and encourages you to **be the business that everyone's talking about.**

Enjoy the book!

To your business success!

Mike

Can Your Business Be *Remarkable*?

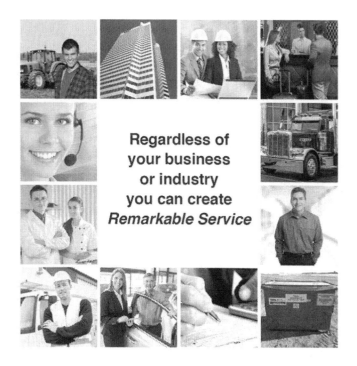

Regardless of
your business
or industry
you can create
Remarkable Service

I know many of you may think that only an elite
hotel or a luxury car dealership can be
remarkable. The reality is that any business in
industry can be *remarkable*.

Here's how:

Farm Equipment Dealership

You may have late hours of operation and 24-hour service for your farming customers during seeding and harvest. If a customer needed a part at 5:00 in the morning, and your team took the call and served the customer, many would say that is *Remarkable Service.*

Legal/Accounting/Financial Services

One of your customers may have an important tax question about their business. They call you and catch you on the eighth hole of a golf course in mid-summer, but you take the call. Many would say that is *Remarkable Service.*

Engineering/Construction

A developer has a big issue with zoning, and they have a deadline to reach in order to get construction underway. Your team works through the weekend to tweak vital details so that they are prepared. Many would say that is *Remarkable Service.*

Call Centre

A young lady calls in about the need to return a pair of shoes that her mother purchased. Your call centre representative discovers that the young lady's mother passed away recently, and there is no receipt for the shoes. You offer a full refund and send a money order to the young lady. When the money arrives via courier, a beautiful bouquet of flowers and a sympathy card is attached. Many would say that is *Remarkable Service*, and the young lady tells hundreds of people about this *remarkable* experience.

Heavy-Duty Truck Dealership

Your business has a customer that operates several trucks in their fleet, and their shop is two hours from your shop. They don't have the time or resources to get a truck in for repairs. Your business sends a team of two to drive to their business and pick up the customer's truck and drive it back to your shop for repairs. The customer sees this as unique and *remarkable* and has five more trucks repaired at your shop.

Health Care

You have a team of Hearing Aid Practitioners, and many of your customers/patients are seniors. A few of them have trouble visiting your office. A team member drives to the patient's house for a hearing test. They stay after the appointment for tea and learn more about the senior patient's family. Some say this is *Remarkable Service*.

Owner/Entrepreneur

You operate a photography studio. One of your customer's children is getting married, and the customer invites you to the wedding. You offer to shoot a complimentary wedding photos, as you will be at the wedding anyway. This saves the young couple thousands of dollars. Some would say this is *remarkable*.

Transportation Business

You have a truck/trailer going to a remote location with your scheduled run that only happens every two months. One of your customers calls your office and asks for two large items that you don't stock (e.g., a fridge and a water cooler). Your sales representative offers to buy the products at a local store and picks them up in his own vehicle. He then gets them on the trailer so that they can be delivered to the remote location. Some would say this is *Remarkable Service*.

Automotive Dealership

A customer of a competing dealership with the same make of vehicle that you sell calls and complains that a trunk liner was damaged the last time that their new car was in your competitor's dealership. The competing dealership refused to repair or replace the damaged trunk liner. You offer to courier a new liner to their address that same day. The customer asks, "How much will that cost?"

You reply, "No cost. After all, you are driving our brand of vehicle, and 'we' value your business." Many would suggest that this is *Remarkable Service*.

Waste Management Service

One of your customers needs a waste bin on an oil and gas site that is 90 minutes away, and the bin is full. It's 2:00 on Friday afternoon, before a long weekend, but there is no scheduled run to this area for 2 weeks. One of your sales representatives loads a bin on his pickup truck that afternoon and offers to deliver it first thing Saturday morning. Some would say this is *Remarkable Service*.

Hospitality Industry

It's 4:45 a.m., and one of your guests calls down to the front desk, as there is no coffee machine in the room. A young man taking the call offers to bring a machine to your guest's room right away. He asks what their favourite coffee is and wants to know if they need something to eat. The guest shares his wish list for coffee and an early-morning breakfast. Ten minutes later, the machine arrives with all promised coffee and food. Later that morning, the guest checks out and discovers that the room service charge, which he expected to have on his bill, is nowhere to be found. Some would suggest that this is *Remarkable Service*.

Crane Company

You do a large lift job for a customer and damage an expensive piece of their equipment because your crane didn't have the lift capacity for this particular lift. You drive back to your shop that is four hours away and bring out a larger crane the next day to finish the lift and make it right. You don't bill your customer for the additional lift and significantly reduce the bill on the original lift. Some may say that this is *Remarkable Service*.

Why More Businesses Don't Create *Remarkable Service*

There are a number of reasons why more businesses don't provide *Remarkable Service*. First of all, **they don't pay enough attention to improving their service or building stronger relationships with their customers.** (It's like a marriage that ends, and one spouse says to the other, "It's wasn't bad, but I really don't feel like making it good again.") It's easy to get complacent when no one is really too unhappy about anything. Often times, business owners and their employees go about business and assume that all is well (or at least HOPE that all is well). If it isn't going well, they may avoid talking about it, as it only happens once in a while. Maybe their service isn't bad, but it's definitely not *remarkable*.

The other aspect is that businesses are just too busy. Day in and day out, we do our best to support customers, but are we spending enough time working "on" the business to improve customer service? Most businesses don't spend enough time working "on" their business. You need to see how your business is delivering service, and ideally see it from your customers' eyes. Working in our business, I am constantly looking at every customer service experience that I encounter. If I go to the gym, and the front desk staff don't even look up at me when I walk by, I think, "You just don't get it." This is not hard! Take a five-second glance at your customer and say, "Good morning."

When was the last time that you looked at all aspects of your business from the perspective of your customers? This may not be a common thing that most business owners or leaders do. Some do a good job of structured customer surveys that offer tangible feedback, but many don't have a process in place to obtain feedback.

Part of our service offering at X5 Management is to see the win-win in customer service. It has to be a win for the business and a win for the customer as well. Businesses have to demonstrate value; deliver great products; and provide excellent, timely customer service. This is essential to having customers come back to your business in any industry.

Another reason businesses are not creating *Remarkable Service* is because they don't invest in **training their people**. They may not know how to properly train someone in customer service. They may train new employees for only a few days, and then the employee is serving customers. They may not have strong soft skills, like communication skills, or know how to effectively deal with conflict when it happens. The reality is that every time a problem arises, employees seem to run to their supervisors or managers for help, or they simply tell their customers that they can't help them. They don't grow and develop more effective ways to serve customers.

An Adventurous Tale of Little to Zero Training

On a past vacation to Mexico, my wife and I decided to do an excursion and experience some adventure. It was a ride in the jungle with some ATVs, and then boating, with some planned snorkeling as well. The trip was not cheap at $360 USD for the two of us, but the agency booking our trip did a great job of explaining and selling the day-long trip, and we were sold. The next morning, we were up early and ready for the adventurous experience.

When we left the hotel, we had about a one-hour ride in a van. The trip was fine, as we had a tour guide who explained some details as to what was happening today, and things seem to be good. We joined the remaining group members at our destination, where we were all going to get on the ATVs. There were about 23 of us in total. The lead excursion guide was giving us details on what was going to occur for our day trip. We had to drive about 90 minutes one way with our ATV side-by-side vehicles in the jungle, going through some off-roading. It sounded pretty cool.

As we were preparing to go, he needed to make sure that all of us were experienced and capable to operate and drive the ATVs, and so he was required to do a driving orientation with each driver. It was now my turn for orientation, as I would be the driver of our ATV. The tour guide walked up beside the ATV and said, "Do you know how to drive?" I said yes, and he said, "Good." Well, apparently, that was the end of my driving lessons, and we were good to go.

We headed down the road onto the highway and started to reach rougher roads full of potholes. We continued on and later learned that this was the off-roading. One passenger of our ATV said to us, "This isn't off-roading; this is just driving on a very bad road." LOL! It was full of potholes, mud, and water.

In light of the fact that we had extra passengers in the back seat of our ATV, I was driving a little bit slower. I asked them if they were open to going a little bit faster where we can even get wet and muddy, driving through the water, and they were okay with that idea.

As we entered our third or fourth major mud waterhole, the engine in our ATV became wet, and all of a sudden it was sputtering and crawling along at a snail's pace. The engine light came on, and we thought, "Great, we are not going to enjoy the day ahead!!"

Inevitably, our vehicle stalled, and we had to dry it out for a while ... parked in the middle of nowhere. Not too concerning, however, one thing was obvious: No one was waiting for us, as there was no tour guide behind us (as promised at the start of our tour). Everyone in our group, including the two guides, were way ahead of us, and we didn't exactly know how far ahead of us.

Thirty to forty-five minutes later, we were back on the road, rolling along and going as fast as we could. Finally, we came upon the remainder of the group while they were stopped for some sightseeing. We had a bit of a chat, explaining that we had vehicle problems, but they didn't seem to care too much about that.

We had another 30 minutes to drive before lunch, but we made it through to our destination. When we arrived at a small village where we were going to have lunch, I decided to pull the lead tour guide member to the side and explain to him about our issue and concerns for our return trip, as our ATV would be slow going back to the van later on in the day. Somewhere in our conversation, I had asked how long he had been doing this job, and he said, **"I've been on the job four days."** Wow! Four days doesn't seem like a lot of time, and my guess was he had little to zero training and orientation. It was pretty obvious. His leadership and customer-service savvy was not impressive and non-existent. Apparently, we weren't the only customers that were upset. We could overhear some people from another country (I believe they were from Spain) as they talked in Spanish and were challenging the lead tour guide about what was going on. He didn't seem to care too much about their concerns, either.

Now it's time to get on the boats and do some touring. We spotted some dolphins and turtles, which proved to be an entertaining part of the trip. The weather was amazing, and then it was time to go snorkelling.

The lead guide shocked us with news and poor customer service. He said, "Unfortunately, we can't go snorkelling today!" Everyone was surprised and angry, asking him why. He said, "We have certain regulations, and we can't go snorkelling today." I thought to myself, "We can't go snorkelling today because it's nice and sunny, the water's calm, or were there other reasons?"

As I think back, I'm not even sure I ever noticed any snorkelling gear anywhere on any boat. Were we really going snorkelling ... who knows?

It was now time to head back to land and get ready to drive our ATVs and make that two-hour-plus trek back to where our van was parked, through the jungle and through the rough roads, mud, and water. Would our ATV stall again?

We had some concerns because we saw the sun was starting to go down, we still had two hours of driving, and we continued to have ATV problems. We were going to be really behind, and the reality is, no one was going to wait for us; in fact, no one would likely care.

As predicted, we did have some vehicle problems again, but we had a different strategy this time. We were driving very slowly through the water to prevent our engine from stalling, but when it was dry and rough, we went full tilt to try to make up some time.

Our final 35 minutes of the tour ended in a small village, and we had to drive through town, but here's the catch: No one was around again, and **we were all by ourselves in the dark, not really knowing exactly where we had to go**, and so we had to guess what road to take. Was this the adventure that we were looking for?

Finally, we arrived back at our starting point, where our van was parked and we had to drop off the ATV, and by this time most of the group had already gone.

There was only a small group remaining, including the Spanish-speaking tourists, and they were ripping into the lead tour guide along with his boss, who was at the checkpoint. We heard the word **refund** and thought, "REFUND? Yeah, right, they are going to give us a refund ... not likely." But, as a few people continued to argue with them, they were starting to buckle, and a young lady was helping to try and calm the customers and resolve the situation with some possible solutions.

She said to us, "You are going to have to contact your agent back at your hotel or resort and get a refund."

I decided to slowly approach her in a kinder, gentler manner and didn't raise my voice. I asked her, "Please explain to us exactly how that's going to happen and how we are going to get a refund?"

She seemed stunned by that question, and her stutter-step response suggested she really didn't have a plan. She looked at all of us and said, "I will call them now." To make sure that she was calling them (the agency back at the resort), we went into her trailer as well and listened to her phone call. While it was in Spanish, I relied on the tourists who spoke Spanish to understand exactly what was being said. After the call, more and more people who remained (probably only one third of the group) actually started to receive refunds. Now, it was our turn, and I stood patiently and waited as she handed me over $360 of cold, hard U.S. cash. I was shocked, but pleased. As we were preparing to leave, I asked the lead tour guide about what he would do differently for the next tour. He replied, "I don't know or care because I am quitting tonight."

This particular trip proved to be somewhat challenging and even potentially dangerous, but ironically it gave us a lot to talk about when we returned from our vacation. It definitely made for some interesting content for this book to illustrate the power of training and effectively teaching and coaching people on how to deal with challenging situations, difficult customers, and how to be a leader when it comes to customer service.

While this trip and story happened in Mexico, it could have happened in Canada, the United States, or it could have happened in Finland; it doesn't matter. The point is this: If you don't train your people and prepare them for effective customer service and give your customers good service experiences, your business will have major problems, including a loss of business.

The reality is that not all of us are going on excursions like this every day, but many of us go to stores or places of business every day. Whether it's the grocery store, the dry cleaner, the bank, or the car dealership, it doesn't matter. Are the employees of those companies trained to serve you? Do they **leave you in the dark and on your own?** What about your business? Is your team really trained?

As I wrote this story about the Mexican excursion, it hit me hard! While this story is true, and has some humour to it, the sad reality is that it is closer to a daily occurrence for so many businesses that it was a real eye-opener for me.

- How many businesses overpromise and under-deliver?

- How many don't communicate and keep customers in the dark?

- How many don't really care about your experience?

- How many businesses can afford to give a full refund to every other customer?

In my experience, this happens far too often, and the only thing that is *remarkable* is the story that is told after you disappoint the customer (the Remarkably Bad Story about Service)! Let's hope it is not a bad story about your business, or mine!!

A final comment about a lack of training for employees: It is my belief that you can teach an old dog a new trick. I often hear stories that a business may not invest in someone because they have worked for the business for 20 years and are 40, 50, or 60 years of age and are set in their ways. While it may be true and a reality, I usually discover that the individuals in question never had any significant amount of structured training in their entire careers. This is very unfortunate, but the good news is, when they do get some training, because their employer decides to invest in them (sometimes at our recommendation and suggestion), the employee responds very well to the tailored training and coaching and improves very quickly.

The other challenge for businesses is that they may rush the hiring process and hire the wrong people. When times are busy and the talent pool is scarce, many businesses rush the hiring process and look for a warm pulse rather than the best candidate. This rarely works in the short or long-term for both the business and the employee, and your customers pay the price for this decision.

A few months ago, I was speaking to a business connection of mine, who is a very well respected business owner in Western Canada. He is able to travel a lot and enjoy life while his business continues to thrive in the good times and in the more challenging times. He told me, "Mike, I have **the best people in the world working for our business**, and I only hire the best." While it is hard to verify if he actually has the "best" people in the world, one thing is hard to deny: His business thrives all the time and has been around for many, many years. If you want the best, don't rush the hiring process!

Food for thought: Many strong and forward-thinking business owners and leaders should consider that when a downturn occurs, it's a time to plan to upgrade their talent pool. While this is a tough decision to make, it allows their business a tremendous opportunity to hire when more time is allowed in the process and they have the ability to hire better people and ideally the best people, simply because more of them may be available in the market.

While this may seem like a cold and unfair decision, it is a very important decision for their business and the future.

Let's compare it to sports. Hockey teams do this all the time. When a strong team is making a run for the playoffs and ideally achieve their desired goal of a Stanley Cup, they trade players (i.e. upgrade the talent pool). They want the best players on their team to allow them the opportunity to achieve maximum success. Business leaders should think the same way. If your business plans on being open in the long run and continue to grow and prosper, it is key to upgrade your talent pool, particularly when the talent is more readily available.

One final aspect in this chapter for you to consider:

Businesses usually don't focus on the little things that can make their service *remarkable.* Most customers truly appreciate the little things.

Did we greet them by name?

Was the promised delivery time of a product or service ready earlier than expected?

Did we actually take the time to call the customer to tell them that their product was ready early?

Did we smile at the customer and acknowledge them? Such small, "little things", but so significant in any business. When times are good and customers walk in the door and pay any price, life may be good to your business. However, what happens when times are tough and the economy is challenged with economic hardship, or new and aggressive competitors are opening across the street? Most businesses may resort to cutting prices, but rarely do they concentrate on improving their customer service.

Here's a quick example to illustrate this point. I was out for dinner with my wife at Corso 32, one of the top-rated restaurants in our city of Edmonton. The place was packed, and reservations were made weeks in advance—if not months in some cases—to get a table. The dining experience from the front door to the kitchen was *remarkable*. They treat you like you are entering their home and make every step of the dining experience memorable and *remarkable*. While the price is steep, you do get what you pay for. They are extremely good at what they do, and customers keep coming back. The economy may be down or up, but the customers pack the restaurant. High-quality service and excellent food win the day in their case.

On the flip side of this story, a friend of mine who also lives in Edmonton bought a second home in Arizona. Having a home in Arizona is a great idea for the cold weather that we have for six months or more in Edmonton. After my friend got into his new home, he had to do some shopping to stock his house with furniture and appliances. He went to a well-known store, which I'll leave unnamed to be nice. He bought a washer and dryer, along with a fridge and a stove package. He arranged delivery while in Arizona because he was only there for one week due to work commitments back home. The delivery truck arrived with the washer, dryer, and stove. "Where's the fridge?" my friend asked.

The delivery driver told him, "I guess they didn't load it on the truck."

My friend said to him, "Well, you have to go back

and get it," and the driver replied, "We can't because we're fully booked with deliveries this week." My friend immediately called the store and voiced his frustration, and they replied with the same, "No delivery this week. Sorry."

As you can imagine, my friend's frustration hit another level (*S&@!x.), so he drove down to the store and talked to his sales representative. Once again, he was given the same "No can do" answer.

My friend escalated his complaint to the store

manager. Again, he received the same response. By now the volume of his tone was significantly louder, and he was asked to **keep it down**, but he didn't tone it down. He tried to explain that he was only in Arizona for a few days and a delivery next week was not an option, but they still didn't want to help. He then asked for his money back on the fridge so that he could go to another store to buy one, and, believe it or not, they refused to give him his money back. Finally, after more yelling and persistence from my friend, the manager of the store offered this less-than-*remarkable* solution: "You can rent a truck on your own, and we will load the fridge here, but you have to unload it yourself." **Unbelievable!!** My friend ended up renting a truck and getting his new neighbours to help him unload the fridge in Arizona. Wow! This is not how you service what you sell.

The moral of the story is, don't let your fridge stand alone in the cold. When you buy a fridge and stove, make sure you ask if they are going to be delivered on the same day.

When I hear a story like the one I just described, it frustrates me. I shake my head, and I think, "How would I have handled this customer service disaster if I worked for the store in question?" Stories like this demonstrate why I am passionate about how we can endeavour to help our customers by improving service. Ultimately, it's about *People and Process.* The right people following the right process, but they are empowered and have the ability to make the right decisions when required!

Now, I know that in some cases customers can be totally unreasonable with their demands, but more times than not, common sense wins the day with your customer. It is my hope that this book will make everyone look at the opportunity to achieve *Remarkable Service* in a different light and believe that it is actually possible and not that difficult or complicated.

While the word **"remarkable"** is not new, it aligns well with my belief that customer service can be *remarkable*. But what does *remarkable* mean exactly? Does your business do something that your customers would "remark" about? It doesn't have to be big, but it can be memorable and impactful enough to your customer so that they will tell other people, and they may tell lots of people in some situations. That could be a good story or a bad story, like the ones I shared earlier.

A good example: I have a weekly dry-cleaning routine, and I have gone to the same business in Edmonton, Riverbend Dry Cleaners, for years. Every time I go in, all the team members of the store greet me by name. You may say that this is not *remarkable,* but there's more. Half the time I go into the store; they have my dry cleaning hanging at the counter when I arrive simply because they see my car pull up in front of the store. I find this simple act *remarkable*. In fact, I share this story often, as I feel this is *remarkable* because I *remark* about it all the time.

Remarkable can be simple, and it doesn't have to cost your business a lot of money. I want everyone who reads this book to look at their business with a different view. I want to create awareness that a service challenge may exist in your business and encourage you to do something about it, to think like your customers, and perhaps see that your customer service delivery/approach could be much better.

Why the Little Things Make All the Difference

Businesses that provide *Remarkable Service* tend to have happier and more satisfied customers who tell others about their service. Ultimately, that creates stronger loyalty, and it can enhance the ability to ask for more referrals or recommendations. As a general rule, their businesses run more smoothly. Their teams are more engaged and helpful, they retain great people, and they are able to weed out the poor performers. They likely have better sales/revenue than a business without *Remarkable Service*, and the customers tend to be less price sensitive when they get *Remarkable Service.* The team working at a business with *Remarkable Service* likely has some extra passion to make it all about the customer, and they love what they do. Customers tend to remark about the little things, and there is usually a consistent theme, and consistency can win the day when it comes to creating *Remarkable Service.*

I always enjoy singing the praises about Lexus of Edmonton. For Lexus of Edmonton, it's about the little things. I'm very blessed to call Bruce Kirkland, Dealer Principal at Lexus of Edmonton, a dear friend. I'm in awe of his community support and how he continually instills excellence in his team by delivering *Remarkable Service* to their valued customers at Lexus of Edmonton. During an interview with our business, X5 Management, Bruce shared his perspective on customer service excellence.

Bruce Kirkland, Lexus of Edmonton

Here is how that interview went:

X5: Are there one or two things that are extremely important in maintaining a high level of customer service?

Bruce: I really think that there are not just one or two things because I really believe it's a puzzle, and you have to put the puzzle together to make it go correctly. I would say a couple things. First is to hire correctly. Lexus of Edmonton has this amazing culture of customer service and relationships. We hire very carefully to protect our culture, and I'm not afraid to hire people who have no car experience. In fact, I'd rather hire people without any car experience. If someone has been in the customer service business somewhere else, those skills are transferable. A lot of people are afraid to do that.

Second, you have to make sure the people you hire have pride in what you do. We make sure that everyone in our dealership knows what's expected of him or her, so we have to communicate with them clearly. You have to make sure that they're involved in the process of why we're doing what we're doing, not just telling them to be nice. It's a long process, but hire correctly. Make sure they are trained correctly.

X5: How do you get that team of people involved and maintain your focus on customer service?

Bruce: A couple of things have to happen: It can't be top down. If it's top down, it's not going to work. We do many things at Lexus of Edmonton. One of the things that I am particularly proud of is called *Opportunities and Challenges*. Every year the management team gets together and looks at all opportunities and challenges. Every year we ask each department to do the same thing, so these people come up with opportunities and challenges, and they become engaged in that process. They come up with a lot of opportunities and challenges, and I think that's really important that it's grassroots up, and our people are really happy to be involved. Top down doesn't work with any organization, so make sure they're engaged. Make sure you train them. A lot of times in our industry (or any industry), we tell people to do their jobs, but we don't train them. Just go do this! We believe in internal training, and we believe in external training. Training is key to our success!

We call people guests. We don't call them customers because we treat people like they are in our house. At Lexus of Edmonton, we call them guests because how would you like to be treated in our house? Little things like walking them to the door. Greet them! It's the little things that make the biggest differences for sure.

Every point of contact is critical for success of customer service. It's not just selling the car; that's the easy part. It's how they are greeted when they come in to the business. How does reception treat them? The two most important people in my dealership are reception and detailing. Some people come in here and say the car is great, but it's dirty, so every point of contact is absolutely critical, and I think sometimes in our business we forget about that.

I always say here: Under-promise and over-deliver. If we can under-promise and over-deliver and wow them, then it's way better than overpromising and not delivering. I think every point of contact in your business is critical, so don't forget about the people you don't think need training. The whole staff needs training; not just management needs training. It's great that managers are trained, but I think the entire team needs training. If you do that, they're going to be engaged.

Spend money on training. It makes your staff better. You are investing in them, and they feel you are investing in them. They're going to want to do it. They're going to take pride in working here and making sure that they could do that.

You have to empower them. A lot of companies don't empower people. I empower my staff to make decisions. They don't have to run to me to make a decision, so make a decision. If that decision is the best for the customer, then let's make that decision; let's not wait around and have to go through three layers to make a decision.

X5: How do you actively manage the customer experience?

Bruce: It's a little more difficult to manage it all, but if your team is trained right, then you will be fine.

We do all sorts of different things here because we really believe that it's the whole experience in any company. I tell my team, don't worry about the car; the car will take care of itself. Let's worry about the people in front of us. It's what we call the whole Lexus experience. It's the little things that we do. We have many events for our guests, anything from wine-tasting events for all guests or Ladies Night at a great restaurant, where we buy them dinner. We do these things to keep them engaged and to experience WOW!

At Christmas we make sure they have a little gift on the car seat when they come in. Little things make a big difference. You don't think they're big because it's this beautiful car, but it's the little things that they're just wowed by. I think one of the things we forget is that it doesn't have to be big; sometimes it just is a little thing that really makes your guests very happy.

Your staff has to be engaged. We have great pride here.

Lexus has a competition, and every month we review that with our staff. It's called *The Pursuit of Excellence*. It's a competition among all the dealers in Canada. At the start of every month, we have a kick-off meeting and explain where we are and what we need to work on. **We're fortunate that we have an amazing team and have won this nine years in a row.** We always have a BIG celebration.

I think also that you just have to look after people. We have to reward people when they do good jobs. We have an internal reward system, and when someone does something well, we recognize and reward him or her.

I get way too much credit: My staff does all the work, and it's really my staff that have done all the work, and you know that they buy into it.

We're very proud, and the *Pursuit of Excellence* is an amazing thing, but you have to communicate with your staff. When you're in a leadership position, if you don't communicate with your staff and talk to them, you're not going to be successful. I have to make sure that I do what I expect them to do, and it starts at the top.

We do the little things really well. We have a newsletter called *The Little Things* that goes out each month because it's the little things that are going to make the big difference. We do the big things really well. Most companies do the big things well. It's the little things that they miss.

We are really blessed at Lexus of Edmonton. I am very proud of the team and the jobs they do. It separates us—we're different.

This interview is a brilliant example of *Remarkable Service*, and I just had to include it in the book because most businesses can adopt the principles that Bruce has talked about at Lexus of Edmonton. As you can see, it's the little things that make the difference, as Bruce says again and again in this interview. When business owners, leaders, and managers read this book, I want them to **think about the little things** that make all the difference. From our perspective at X5 Management, it's the little things that we do to help businesses—and making those little things consistent—that form business success for our customers.

Take a moment now to list the little things that your business does really well.

Our Top 5 List of Little Things We Do Well

1. _____

2. _____

3. _____

4. _____

5. _____

Our Top 5 Little Things to Improve Upon

1. _____

2. _____

3. _____

4. _____

5. _____

Customer = King
(Don't Let the King Leave the Building)

Elvis Presley is still regarded as the "King of Rock 'n' Roll," and through his career it became a standard line from his show for announcers to say that Elvis, AKA "The King," had left the building. (Meaning: The show is over; go home. He wasn't coming back for an encore.) It is still used to indicate that someone has made an exit or that something is complete.

If **CUSTOMER = KING**, what does it mean when your customer leaves your building or business?

Does it mean that they left your business feeling happy, satisfied, or fulfilled? Does it mean that something is complete (*Remarkable* Customer Satisfaction)? Does it mean they left your business and won't be back for an encore (another appearance)?

A year or two ago, I had a customer service experience that was less than stellar. I'll call this business **"Less than Stellar Business Inc."** (I changed the name to protect the innocent.) They allowed me the opportunity to leave their business, and I must admit that I didn't feel like a king. Ironically, I wasn't even looking to be treated like a king. I simply wanted to receive reasonable service for reasonable pay, but nope, this didn't happen. All aspects of the "almost" sales and service process were poor. I say "almost," as they didn't get my money. I left before things went too far. In other words, I decided to walk away and avoid further disappointment. Sadly, no one was running to the door to save my business.

Does **Customer = King in your Business?**

In my opinion, if your business is looking to grow revenue, offer more products and services to your customers, gain more customers, then your "customer" must be king. While being a king is all about royalty, being a customer is all about loyalty!

How to treat your customer like a king?

Be Remarkable. Give your customer something "great" to talk about.

Assess your moments of truth from your customer's eyes (e.g. greetings, smiles, cleanliness of your business, etc.)

How would you rate this area?

(Poor) 0---1---2---3---4---5 (Remarkable)

How could you improve this rating?

_____

_____

_____

Determine the Lifetime Value of your customer (i.e. revenue/transactions; transactions/year; revenue/year; # of years that customer will be "your" customer; customer lifetime value; likelihood of "great" and remarkable service keeping your customer).

(Poor) 0---1---2---3---4---5 (Remarkable)

How could you improve this rating?

_____

_____

_____

As mentioned earlier, I am a customer at a dry cleaning store. Let's look at the lifetime value of my business to that store as a customer. I spend $30 to $40 in a given week on dry cleaning. If I do that 50 weeks a year, $40/week x 50 weeks = $2,000 of business per year. You get a pretty quick number of what I'm worth to that business as a customer in one year. Now, what if I'm a customer for seven or eight years, like I've been? What if I'm a customer for another 10 years: 10 x

$2,000 = $20,000. The lifetime value of one average customer like me, Mike Mack, is valuable, and I want businesses and their employees to understand the lifetime value of all of their customers. Not just the big customers, but the average customers—and I say average just based on average revenue/sale—and the smaller customers, who still spend some valued money within a business, which is important.

Another question we spend a lot of time addressing is, "What is the cost of poor service?" I've talked earlier about the lifetime value of a customer, but what's the cost of poor service? There are many examples, such as a return phone call that doesn't happen for a quote for a particular product. I can think of an example where I had requested a quote on a $400 part for my vehicle, and they never called me back with a price. The cost of poor service in that case was the entire amount of the purchase—they didn't get my business. Their competitor did!

I want your business to understand what the cost of poor service can be and how that can impact your business.

Determine the cost of poor service. How many people will an "upset" customer tell about your poor service? How does your business rate this area?

(Poor) 0---1---2---3---4---5 (Remarkable)

How could you improve this rating?

_____

_____

_____

Assess your Service: Reliability (consistency); responsiveness (to requests and complaints); speed (of everything your business does); competence (skilled, trained, and knowledgeable employees); value (service to price ratio); friendly (personable, smiling).

(Poor) 0---1---2---3---4---5 (Remarkable)

How could you improve this rating?

_____

_____

_____

Determine the "behaviours" to support remarkable customer service for your business.

These simple tips may prevent "The King" AKA "customer" from leaving your business.

(Poor) 0---1---2---3---4---5 (Remarkable)

How could you improve this rating?

_____

_____

_____

Everyone Communicates, but Does Everyone Connect?

As I have learned from leadership guru and best-selling author, John C. Maxwell, "...connecting is all about others."

As Maxwell stated in his book: *Everyone Communicates—Few Connect,* "When you are trying to connect with people, it's not about you —it's about them. If you want to connect with others, you have to get over yourself."

How can you apply this in business? Whether it is trying to sell something to a prospective customer, servicing an existing customer, or speaking to your team or an audience, there is a need for connection. Ask great questions, make your message about them, and listen more and talk less!

This topic gains lots of focus in our business at X5 Management. Whether we are working with a sales team, business leaders, or a corporate audience, the opportunity to improve communication is ongoing, and that is why we support sales and service teams to "turn soft skills into hard assets."

Photo Credit: Avonlea Photography

Everyone has a unique style of communication, and there are many communication profiles/assessments that are available in the marketplace (e.g., HRDQ: What's My Communication Style).

If you can leverage your communication style strengths and be mindful of potential communication trouble spots, you have a better chance of connecting with others.

"Connecting is the ability to identify with people and relate to them in a way that increases your influence with them," says Maxwell.

Three Questions People Are Asking About You, according to John C. Maxwell:

1. Do you care for me?

2. Can you help me?

3. Can I trust you?

How do you communicate that you care for your customers?

_____

_____

_____

How do you communicate when you are helping a customer?

_____

_____

_____

What are the various ways that you communicate/instill trust with your customers?

_____

_____

_____

No Worries, Mr. Mack, That Becomes My Problem.

This story took place more than 20 years ago, and I still tell it because it was that *remarkable*.

In a previous career within the Financial Services Industry, I spent three years working in Prince George, British Columbia. One of my favourite restaurants was called DaMarinos, a delightful little Italian restaurant with amazing food and *Remarkable Service*. Their spaghetti carbonara was amazing!! On one particular lunch hour, I brought a few colleagues with me who were in town from Vancouver, and we were hungry, but we arrived during the start of the lunch-hour rush.

As I entered the restaurant, my favourite waiter promptly greeted me at the door. "Good day, Mr. Mack, how are you today?" I told him I was great.

He responded, "Do you have reservations?"

I sheepishly

replied, "No, sorry, we didn't know our lunch schedule and plans today."

He replied, **"No worries, Mr. Mack, that becomes my problem."**

WOW!!!!!! That was one of the most *remarkable* lines that I have ever heard from a customer service perspective, ever! I was totally delighted, and that *Remarkable Service* was so memorable that I continue to tell this story all the time!

When was the last time that you made your customer's problem, your problem? Did you collaborate on a win-win solution?

What does *Remarkable Service* mean to you? When was the last time that you experienced *Remarkable Service*? Ideally, it is good and above-and-beyond, but it doesn't have to be big.

As you are out and about today, see if you can observe *Remarkable Service.* If you are working in your place of business, try to deliver *Remarkable Service.*

Remarkable Service is wonderful to receive and not as difficult to give as you might think.

The Key Mistakes to Avoid

There are a few key mistakes companies make which contribute to poor or unremarkable service. In fact, it's a bit ironic that a lot of businesses feel that they provide great customer service, but the reason they feel that way is because they don't really ask their customers. That's the first mistake I see businesses make.

1. They don't take the time to have a proper mechanism to get valuable, concrete feedback on customer service. Did they ask if their customers were happy with their service and how it could be improved?

2. They turn a blind eye on customer service issues that occur in their business. Find out if they are a one-off or if this situation happens often. Get on top of it, and ideally ensure that it doesn't happen again.

3. They don't track status of issues and resolve customer service issues. When customer service issues occur, and they will, you must ensure that things don't fall through the cracks. When did we say that we would get back to the customer? Who committed what to the customer? These are all key aspects to resolve a customer service problem.

4. We don't inspect what we expect with our employees. Perhaps a new employee was

instructed to do something to support a customer. Did you follow-up (i.e. inspect) to make sure that it was done? You don't have to do this forever, but you must first trust that it is going to get done and that you have processes in place to consistently get it done.

5. There is a lack of defined role clarity. Who should do what when it comes to customer service, and particularly when resolving an issue? Too often, we hear things like, "That wasn't my job; I thought it was yours," or, "I assumed you were going to do that." Take the time to define functional roles and the associated duties and tasks that go with those roles.

Five Points that Lead to *Remarkable*

Number one, and while this is very simple, it's key: **Be nice**, and earn your customer's respect. Whether it's a phone or in-person greeting or a conflict with a customer, you have to be nice and show patience in order to earn their respect. You have to manage your emotional intelligence and keep calm. As the old saying goes, "The customer is always right," and we at least have to create the perception that the customer is right because they have the right to voice their concerns or be unhappy with your particular service. This is a must! If you walk into a place of business and people are grumpy, rude, or defensive, and don't treat you well, it will likely be a key factor in whether or not you will return to that place of business again in the future.

What being nice looks like:

- Greet customers; say hello or welcome them into your place of business. ☺

- Make eye contact, and acknowledge them.

- When a service challenge occurs (and it will), be nice when resolving the issues. Don't try and prove the customer wrong!

What being nice doesn't look like:

- Being rude or condescending: "I know everything, and this customer is an idiot."

- Talking about the last customer you served in front of the current customer that you are working with. (This drives me crazy, and I see it far too often. I may be getting ready to pay for my groceries at a checkout counter, and one cashier will say something to another cashier, such as: "Wow, was that last guy ever slow. I don't think he could count to 10." I think to myself, "I sure hope that I don't do anything out of order, or they will talk about me, too.")

- Not giving your customers the time of day and making them feel like they are an inconvenience.

- When a service challenge arises, being confrontational and defending your position and proving your customer wrong, even at the risk of losing the customer.

The second component is **demonstrating value**. We think a lot about demonstrating value in our business at X5 Management, as we are in the professional services business. Demonstrating value for us **must** occur before our customers cut the cheque to our business. Demonstrating value may include your past track record and how you actually supported and assisted customers, improving their service levels. If you have demonstrated value, you may earn the right to ask for testimonials, recommendations, and referrals. Demonstrating value is key and critical.

What would your customers say about the value that they receive from your business? Are they getting their monies' worth?

What demonstrating value may look like:

- Offer to meet the customer or prospect when it is most convenient for them.

- Provide valuable tips and insight, and don't expect to be compensated for this at the outset of the relationship.

- Ask great questions before making any attempt to sell a customer/prospect on your product or service. Make it all about them.

- Earn trust before earning the sale.

- Show the benefits that your services have provided other customers.

What demonstrating value may not look like?

- Making it more about you than the customer.

- Being inflexible to customer requirements.

- Selling-Selling-Selling and avoiding truly listening and understanding what the customer/prospect wants.

The third component is **reliability.** That old saying, "Do what you say you're going to do," still holds true today in business in any industry, anywhere. Be reliable. Even if you can't deliver exactly what the customer's expectations were, be reliable enough to give them a heads-up on that, e.g., "Your truck is not going to be ready on Friday morning—it's going to be ready *late* Friday afternoon," and then honour your word at that point in time. Being reliable is critical. In doing so, you must always tell all of your employees exactly what was committed to your customer. If someone is missed in the process, a key step could go unnoticed and, we fail to deliver on our promise. Even if only one employee makes the mistake/error, your business could be seen as unreliable in the eyes of your customer.

What being reliable may look like:

- Do what you said that you would do.

- Under-promise and over-deliver.

What being reliable may not look like?

- Overpromising and under delivering, just to keep the customer from complaining more.

- Not returning customer calls/emails in a timely manner.

The fourth component, as I have alluded to earlier, is investing the time and resources to **train employees**. More importantly, you need a process to train your team. Is it technical training or soft-skills training? Both are key and critical.

Who will train employees? Will it be a designated person who is well versed in the technical training and who is good at training and coaching others? Some training and coaching may occur by a third-party provider.

What trained employees may say and do:

- They feel empowered and engaged and make good decisions.

- They buy in to company vision and direction.

- They deliver *Remarkable Service.*

What untrained employees may say and do:

- They develop a sense of apathy. (They don't care; it's only a job.)

- They lack confidence and competence.

- They avoid making decisions that are key to customer service and retention of customers.

The final point for any business is **communicating** with your customer when challenges arise or to simply stay connected and build trust and rapport. This seems to come up all the time. When we have an issue, we might try to avoid the issue rather than directly communicating with customers and updating them about the fact that, things aren't going as we had hoped. It's like an airline. If we're travelling, it's nice to know if the flight is late.

We're not happy about it, but it's good to know because we can change our schedules accordingly. Communicating with your customer when challenges arise is critical to business success. Communicating with your customers on a regular basis is essential to maintaining a relationship with your business. If you don't communicate, your competitors may be talking to your customers.

There are a number of reasons businesses don't communicate with their customers when there is a challenge:

1. They are just too busy, and they don't have time. (Not a great excuse.)

2. They don't have adequate processes in place to remember to call that customer back when challenges arise. That might be relatively easy for me to do in our business, but if you're a heavy-duty truck dealership, for example, communicating with the customer may need to be assigned to someone else with the appropriate technical expertise. You have to make sure that they phone the customer back in a timely manner.

3. They are complacent: "Oh well, the customer will probably call us back anyway."

4. The lack of essential and timely information for the customer.

5. They don't like to communicate bad news. If what we're communicating to the customer may disappoint the customer that makes it a bit more difficult.

A very helpful tip to remember when dealing with a customer service issue and conflict arises.

When the relationship with someone is not important and the outcome of the solution is not important, you can avoid the conflict. (e.g. a Disagreement with a stranger, as it is not worth the fight)

When the relationship is important and the outcome of the solution is not "as important" you can compromise. (e.g. settling on a price of a low cost repair and the difference may be a small amount of money. Is it worth losing a customer over $10., $100, or $1,000. depending on your business?)

When the relationship is VERY important (which should be the case with most of your customers) and the outcome of the solution is VERY important you must "collaborate" with your customer. (You must find the win-win in the solution).

Remarkably Good vs. Remarkably Bad

There can be a subtle difference, but when you see it, you will know. I have a keen eye to see the difference, simply because it is part of our business to see the difference. Like a musician that can hear a note played off key, I pay close attention when service is delivered on key (i.e. Remarkably Good) and when it is off the mark (i.e. Remarkably Bad).

I love to use sports analogies from time-to-time to bring home a point. When I noted that there is a subtle difference between Remarkably Good Service and Remarkably Bad Service, it is like losing a one-goal hockey game. It hurts when that happens (Our Edmonton Oilers hockey team know this too well.), but what if it happens way too often? What one or two tweaks to the "game-plan" could have made the difference? Could we have paid more attention to detail? Was it about the "little things" that were missed or forgotten?

Flying high doesn't make me want to smile

As some of you may recall, back in 2000, two major Canadian airlines merged after an acquisition. It was a stressful time for their employees involved, as there was a lot of eventual job redundancy. Some much needed "post merger integration" was required to align this business. Customers/passengers didn't receive a lot of *Remarkable Service* back then, as I recall. I remember this time very well as I travelled regularly from Edmonton to Toronto every other week for months to meet with my boss and other colleagues across the country for regular planning meetings when I was in the Financial Services Industry. On one trip, a former colleague, Al Mactier, was travelling from Victoria, British Columbia to Toronto. He approached the ticket counter to check his baggage. Al noticed an airline representative struggling/arguing with a customer, and when they finished, it was now Al's turn to be served. He could tell she was not happy and totally stressed out with her day. Al was great with customers and always had a big smile, so he looked at the airline representative and said to her, with a grin ☺, "You know, it may help if you smiled at your customers."

Her reply was fast and direct. "SIR, if you had my job, you wouldn't smile either."

Al wittily replied, "You may want to think about getting a different job."

I don't recall how she replied, but hopefully she found her smile again in a new/different job, after the merger.

In today's world, most consumers and businesses are connected in some way to Social Media. Whether it is LinkedIn, Twitter, or Facebook—just to name a few—it is easy to get the word out there. What is the word, exactly? Well, it can be something great about your business or something bad or concerning regarding your business. What businesses need to know is that regardless of their business being active users of Social Media, others can still comment about "your" business. What are they saying? It could be a delightful post about how *remarkable* the business delivered service, or it could be how a customer interaction went wrong and there was a disagreement that a customer didn't like.

I remember a story that a business owner told me a few years back about their business. A situation occurred where a customer was extremely upset about a poor service experience. The customer was a little heated and didn't even wait three minutes after the dialogue with the business ended. They posted a pretty ugly comment on Facebook. The reality was that the story was blown out of proportion, but it didn't matter. The damage was done! The comments spread quickly, and there were 20 or 30 comments from other customers who wanted more details on exactly what took place. Fortunately, the business owner was quick thinking and called the customer who created the original post and was able to diffuse the situation, and the customer agreed to send a follow-up comment to suggest that he overreacted. Wow! You see how quickly this can happen. In the blink of an eye or the click of a post button, bad and concerning news can be spread about your business in seconds. Be careful out there!!

An example of REMARKABLY BAD Service

This story occurred a few years back and was a major catalyst for writing this book. All details are true and accurate.

Someone booked a regular oil change for his vehicle. The plan was to drop off his car at 7:30 a.m. He likes to be early and lined up at the service bay doors at the dealership.

On this particular day he arrived at 7:15 a.m. and was pleased to be the first car lined up. Good news! He would be checked into his appointment right away, and his colleague would pick him up, and they would head off to work.

At 7:30 a.m. he realized that he might not get his wish, as no one was at the dealership in the service department. He knew this to be the case, as the lights were off, and everything was dark, including his mood. It's now 7:41 a.m., and still no sign of anyone. He was getting frustrated and decided to shoot a short video with his smartphone, complete with commentary on this dreadful service experience. (I have viewed this video, and I too was frustrated!!) Finally, at 7:45 a.m. a parking lot attendant noticed him and stopped by the bay door and opened it for the disappointed customer. Ironically, no other customers were in line that day, **not one other customer.** I find that extremely interesting and perhaps a very telling sign about the service at this particular dealership. When he pulled in and parked his car, he walked to the service advisor area. One person was in, and still no other employees were in sight. My friend asked the young man, "Who is the service manager? He stated that he was the manager.

My friend replied, "You know that your service really sucks, as it is now 7:45 a.m., and you supposedly OPEN at 7:30 a.m."

He replied, without a "sorry," by simply saying, "We had a staffing issue today."

My friend quickly replied, "Yes, your staffing issue was due to the fact that no one showed up to work."

Has a similar story happened to you in the past? Is Customer Service an option at a business like this?

Customer Service ❓

(**Groundhog Day:** Approximately eight months later, the exact same thing happened the next time that my friend was at this dealership for regular vehicle servicing! How can you run a business and expect to have customers come back? More importantly, how do you think that many customers of this business remark about the service that they receive? It's UGLY, I'm sure!)

You may have noticed already, but when I reference a *Remarkably* **Good** service story, I will share the name of the company or business with you. It feels great to give them a plug and illustrate how awesome they really are. On the other hand, I always leave out the name of the business that had a *Remarkably* **Bad** service story. Why? Simply because that "bad" business experience could be a one-off or, more importantly, could easily be my business or your business, if we happen to underwhelm a customer at any given time. We need to keep focused and honest that good and bad service is all about perception, and we can be on the bad end of a story in the blink of an eye. **Let's do our part to keep stories about our business** *Remarkably* **Great!**

Case Study:
How to Improve Your Business

A case study that I would like to profile in my book is about a long-time and valued customer, Stahl Peterbilt. They are an Edmonton, Alberta-based truck dealership, and they also have locations in Grand Prairie and Fort McMurray, Alberta.

This business relationship commenced in the spring of 2012. It's hard to believe that it has been that long, and we are fortunate that X5 Management still enjoys an ongoing business relationship with this great organization today.

One of the first projects that Stahl Peterbilt asked us to focus on was specific to their phone system.

The question from Stahl Peterbilt really was less of a technical question about the phone system, but rather how their phone was being used to service and support customer service. X5 Management started in the area of their Parts Department, as they received a high volume of calls on a daily basis. In fact, the volumes were so high at times that it was difficult to keep up with the demand to support the level of customer service that Stahl Peterbilt wanted to maintain, in order to deliver on customer expectations.

The point I want to make here is this particular organization made everything that we did, about the improvement of customer service. Whether it was to improve their people or their process, everything had to be better to keep up with the demands of their customers.

After making several recommendations and completing this project over a three-month period of time, the next project opportunity involved their PDI Centre. PDI stands for "Pre-Delivery Inspection." When a truck is sold—let's say it's intended use will be a cement truck—they need to take the truck chassis and retrofit through one of their strategic partners, called a Body Builder. Body Builders specialize in taking a base truck and adding on all required equipment so that the truck can be used to pour cement in this case. They will send that truck offsite to the Body Builder that actually installs the parts and equipment.

After this process, the truck comes back to the PDI centre. (For the record, Stahl Peterbilt has an offsite PDI centre that is away from its main dealership, so it adds to the complexity of communicating internally and externally with the customer and employees as to where that truck is exactly, in terms of it being finished and ready for delivery to the customer.)

Through the consulting process, we identified that the Sales, Service, and Parts departments were very much a part of this process when the truck was sold, and every customer had specific details or add-ons that they wanted on their truck; the Parts department became very involved in that process after the truck was sold by the Sales team.

As a truck was ready to be serviced in the PDI, Service Technicians, etc. were heavily involved and all of these steps required our involvement for process improvements.

The ultimate outcome for Stahl Peterbilt was that the new process of the offsite location had to be seamless and transparent to the customer so they knew at any given time where the truck was in the process and, more importantly, if it was on track for the projected delivery date

As that project successfully concluded, we moved on to other initiatives specifically around the areas of consulting on process improvements, whether that was in the Service department, the Sales department, or the Parts department.

X5 Management's services continue to evolve in terms of coaching their team because they are very open and receptive to continuous improvement and being better as an organization. For reference, Stahl Peterbilt has been "Best in Class" among all Peterbilt dealerships in North America.

Since late 2014 to the present time, in early 2016, X5 continues to have a lot to do with training and support in the areas of improving sales and service for Stahl Peterbilt. It is interesting that this great organization continually wants to be *remarkable* in all aspects of their business.

Stahl Peterbilt is so committed to the process of improving their already great organization that the people involved in the training and coaching range from receptionists, service technicians, outside part sales team, truck sales team, service advisors, and senior management. An excellent case and example of how a strong business wants to continually improve to be better and add value to their customers. X5 Management is pleased to be part of that improvement process.

"We have made a significant investment in our people and process improvements utilizing the services of X5 Management, with the objective of improving overall Customer Service."
-Eddy Stahl, President, Stahl Peterbilt Inc.

Are You Ready?

My hope is that you think about Customer Service and, more specifically, your Customer Service in a new light. Delivering *Remarkable Service* is not impossible to achieve, but it will take effort and focus.

Take the time to determine what you are committed to improve upon, and plan to focus your time and resources in that direction.

Meet with your team and review some of the questions that were listed in this book and get their input and thoughts.

If you are ready, get started today, as there is no time like the present to focus on improving your business. Your customers will thank you by coming back again and again.

Here's to your *Remarkable Service* Success!

"What is the point of being alive, if you don't at least try to do something Remarkable?"
-John Green

About X5 Management

X5 is a Business Consulting and Coaching firm that specializes in the improvement of sales and service for mid-market businesses.

We offer comprehensive Business Consulting Services, Coaching Services and we have an extensive list of Training and Professional Development courses that are crafted for each business and professionally facilitated. Customers praise our Consulting and Training programs as proven ways to create sales growth and service delivery into *Remarkable Service*. Our relationship-driven approach involves a tailored service model that supports your business's specific needs.

X5 GUARANTEES the satisfaction of its customer. If our customer is not completely satisfied with the value of our services, we will, at the customer's discretion, waive our professional fees or accept a portion of those fees that reflects the customer's level of satisfaction and/or terminate the agreement. Since 2006, we have worked closely with customers in many industries throughout Western Canada. Visit us at:

www.x5management.com

Acknowledgements

I am a very lucky guy to have many wonderful business connections and friends in my world. As I made the decision to write this book, there were many great people and organizations involved behind the scenes in supporting me through the writing and creative process. In addition, I gained valuable insight over my career that allowed me new perspective and greater wisdom. They were all instrumental, and I want to thank each of them with my sincerest gratitude.

Strategic Coach; Bruce Kirkland; Arnold McLaughlin; Bonita Lehmann; Stahl Peterbilt Inc. Matt Graff; Harvey Emas; Ron Dersch; Chad Griffiths; Marilyn Waller; Kamea Zelisko; Susan Mate; Dr. Larry Ohlhauser; 90-Minute Books; Susan Austin; Glen Linton; Elisabeth Rossman; Rick & Lynn Williams; Jeff Polovick; HRDQ; Eden Hampson; Dan Duckering; DEXIO; Peter Kossowan; Vernon Hibbard; Dennis Simpart, and my late parents. (Tony and Helen Mack)

Recommended Reading

Scaling Up-How a few companies make it...and why the rest don't. By: Verne Harnish

The Culture Secret-How to Empower People and Companies No matter what they sell.
By: Dr. David Vik

Mergers & Acquisitions Integration Handbook-Helping Companies Realize the Full Value of Acquisitions. By: Scott C. Whitaker

The Entrepreneurial Roller Coaster – Why now is the time to join the ride. By: Darren Hardy

Built to Sell-Creating a Business that can Thrive without You. By: John Warrilow

Bridges of Trust: Making Accountability Authentic.
By: David Irvine and Jim Reger

Start with Why: How Great Leaders Inspire everyone to Take Action. By: Simon Sinek

Action Steps to *Remarkable Service*

1. Review all aspects of your business that may impact Customer Service.

2. What areas require improvement?

3. How can you improve these areas?

4. Do you know what your customers think and say about your business?

5. Engage your employees in the discussion and listen to their ideas.

6. Gain input, perspective and support from a third-party business advisor on your Customer Service and Sales delivery.

Notes

About the Author

Mike Mack is the founder of X5 Management, an Alberta, Canada-based professional services firm that specializes in improving sales and service for mid-market businesses.

Mike holds an MBA from Athabasca University, along with a Fellow of The Institute of Canadian Bankers designation. Mike is a proud member of Synergy Network (Edmonton), serving as Chair in 2016; ACG (Association for Corporate Growth), serving as Chair and Master of Ceremonies for the Northern Alberta Mergers & Acquisitions Conference in Edmonton, Alberta, March 2016; Member of Toastmasters International, obtaining his Distinguished Toastmasters Designation—DTM. The Distinguished Toastmaster award is the highest Toastmasters International bestows. The DTM recognizes a superior level of achievement in both communication and leadership; Member of CAPS (Canadian Association of Professional Speakers); Past-President, Rotary Club of Edmonton Mayfield (2005/06). Mike and his beautiful partner Bonita live in Edmonton and love biking in Edmonton's River Valley or in the majestic mountains of Alberta.

Connect with Mike

Email:

mike@x5management.com

LinkedIn:
https://ca.linkedin.com/in/mikemackalberta

Twitter:

@x5mike

Made in the USA
Charleston, SC
30 December 2016